ZEN MIND
LIFE THOUGHTS

SCOTT SHAW

Buddha Rose Publications

First Edition 2015

ISBN 10: 1-877792-81-0
ISBN 13: 9781877792816

Library of Congress: 2015931590

Printed in the United States of America

10 9 8 7 6 5 4 3 2 1

ZEN MIND
LIFE THOUGHTS

Introduction

The aphorisms that make up this book were originally composed for the Scott Shaw Zen Blog 4.0, presented on scottshaw.com, between September 2014 and January 2015.

If all you want to do is nothing then
you've already succeeded.

Take a moment, sit down, and calm your mind. Let go of everything you know, understand, or believe.

What are you left with?

If a person creates a position for themselves where you are made to believe that you should listen to what they have to say, they are either lying to you or they are lying to themselves.

You have to look to find.

People never understand the repercussions of their actions until they must pay the price for their actions.

A prayer always equals a desire.

When you read words in books, articles, or on the internet do you only read the words or do you seek the meaning hidden between the words?

If you are the instigator of the chaos you
are responsible for the chaos.

Your action.
Your cause.
Your karma.

The worst sinner is the person who
doesn't consider themselves a sinner.

The rest of your life is defined by this moment. This one right here, right now. What are you doing?

When you have done something that has hurt someone else, how much of your time do you spend thinking about it?

But now, think about this... How much of their time do they spend thinking about it?

Today can be a positive day if you let it be
a positive day.

Why aren't you undoing your doing? Why aren't you fixing the negative things that you have unleashed?

Fixing what you have broken is the ultimate selfless action.

You want to fix your karma, you want to live a better life, then fixing what you have broken is the place to begin.

Every time you say or do something
positive the world gets a little bit better.

Every time you say or do something
negative the world gets a little bit worse.

Can you live without?

Without what?

Only you can answer that.

How many people love you?

How many people hate you?

Why do those who love you, love you?

Why do those who hate you, hate you?

Your life is defined by those who
surround you.

Is your life in order in terms of your finances, your relationships, your health, your emotions, your acquisitions, and your spirituality? If it is, you are responsible. If it is not, you are also responsible.

If anything in your life is out of order, it is you who must set it in order. The longer you wait, the harder it gets.

Once it's done it is never undone.

When was the last time that you consciously did something positive that had a positive effect?

What's on your mind is only in your mind.

Because your past defines your future, what you are doing now will soon be in your past. How will what you are doing now come to define what you want your tomorrow to be?

Is who you used to be keeping you from what you want to become?

If your life is defined by the, *"I am that,"* mentality, what happens when you are not THAT any longer?

You have set the course for your own life in motion. Where you are now is where you deserve to be.

There is always going to be a price to pay.
You just have to decide if you are willing
to pay it.

Never interact with people who do not
have your best interests in mind.

Denying what you did is not the same as undoing what you did.

What you want to be is defined by what
you can be.

The moment you stop lying to yourself
about what you think you should be and
become the person that you can be, then
you are free.

As long as you lie, the lies of others will haunt you.

As long as you claim greatness, there will be people trying to dethrone you.

If you receive from your giving, then you have given nothing at all.

As long as you think of yourself before you think of others, you will never be whole, fulfilled, or truly loved.

The answer to life is easy, stop being something and start being nothing. This is Zen.

When your dreams don't serve you well,
it's time to wake up.

A true leader does not seek followers nor do they demand that people obey what they say. A true leader allows people to come to him or her and decide for themselves what is right or wrong and what they should or should not do.

As long as you lie, the lies of others will haunt you.

As long as you claim greatness, there will be people trying to dethrone you.

If you receive from your giving, then you have given nothing at all.

As long as you think of yourself before you think of others, you will never be whole, fulfilled, or truly loved.

The answer to life is easy, stop being something and start being nothing. This is Zen.

When your dreams don't serve you well,
it's time to wake up.

A true leader does not seek followers nor do they demand that people obey what they say. A true leader allows people to come to him or her and decide for themselves what is right or wrong and what they should or should not do.

If you don't know then you don't know.

What degree do you need to earn to be a psychic, a medium, or a guru?

If you cannot verify a person credentials in the same way as they do in all the valid disciplines, how can you trust what anyone claims to be?

No matter how many times you tell the same lie it never becomes the truth.

If you tell someone that you will do something and you don't do it, there are problems.

If you tell somebody you can do something when you can't do it, there are problems.

If you lie about your ability to do something when you are unable to do it, there are problems.

The only time there is no problems is when you claim nothing, offer no services you cannot provide, and remain perfect within inaction.

An honest person speaks the truth.

An honest person does not speak the truth from their point of view or in a manner that is only defined to make people take their side.

If you present the truth from your point of view, it becomes a lie.

If you let go of the lies, then the truth will engulf you.

When you are angry it is you who is angry.

Does anyone care that you are angry?

What does your anger equal?

If you can step into the simplicity, life becomes so much easier.

When someone is doing something bad that hurts themselves, other people, or the entire world, they do not simply stop out of the goodness of their heart. They only stop when they are forced to stop.

Look around you; who is doing what you are doing? Now, look ahead to people who are thirty, forty, fifty, sixty, seventy years old who have done what you are doing. This will give you insight into what you will become if you continue down the path you are walking upon. For those who are older, look back five, ten, twenty, thirty, forty years. Are you where you should be having done what you are doing? If you are not, who is to blame?

See your life. Imagine you are about to leave this life.

What will you miss the most?

What do you regret the most?

What can you do to correct and fix your mistakes so you will be remembered in a better light?

What can you live the most?

We are each responsible for the ALL of all
that is going on around us.

If you have to ask someone to tell you the truth, they will never tell you the truth. At best they will put their spin on the facts.

Just because it is different doesn't mean it is better.

A lot of differences leads to a lot of problems.

When you enter a new environment do you take the time to listen before you speak or take any action?

Is the soundscape overpowering you or are you overpowering it?

If you are overpowering it, that means you are causing disharmony.

Harmony is the natural state.

Once disharmony is created it is never easily corrected.

Angry people seek out things that will make them angry.

Does a person care what you are feeling when it was they who did something wrong to you?

No, probably not, because they are too busy making up excuses for their actions or telling lies to cover up what they have done.

When was the last time you did
something nice for someone and expected
nothing in return?

Why do you criticize people? Does it make you any more or them any less?

Look for the subtleties.

Most people never take the time to think about how what they are doing today will affect their tomorrow.

Your life is not going to turn out the way you planned. Okay, now what?

Life has nothing to do with the gods, with the abstract energy of the universe promised by the soothsayers, or the false promises claimed by those who declare to have access to the great-beyond. Life is about you getting busy and doing something.

If you are looking for displays of the paranormal, you will find them.

If you are a worldly person and you do worldly things, no one will judge your actions as they are expected.

If you claim to be a spiritual person everything you do will be put under the microscope.

Most people don't care until they are
forced to care.

If you do something good in the name of religion is god or are you to blame?

If you do something bad in the name of religion is god or are you to blame?

Jealousy is never the right emotion.

No matter what you think you are doing,
that is not necessarily what you are doing.

Life is defined not by what you think. Life
is defined by what you do and the impact
it has.

If you are doing for you – if you are doing
because you think you have something to
offer, who is being served? Someone else
or You?

If you are serving you at any level, then no
one else is receiving the benefits of any
service you believe you are providing.

Everybody knows what is right and what is wrong.

Some people are simply too driven by their emotions and their desires to care.

If a person is justifying what they have done, then you know that they know what they did was wrong.

Who do you blame?

People always change their stories after
the reality has been lived.

Everybody has a reason but very few know the reason why.

You have one hour to live. What will you do?

If you live your life from this perspective the things you do will be much more focused and the people you hurt will be far fewer.

There is no one who is good, just as there is no one who is bad. It is only perception.

Is that what you believe?

Who cares!

Why don't you go and tell the truth about yourself.

Believe me, the world will be a better place.

Shatter your compulsions.

Stop your obsessions.

You will be better and the world will be a
better place.

A liar is forever a liar.

A deceiver is forever a deceiver.

A liar forever finds a reason to lie.

A deceiver continues to find reason to continue their deceit.

Be careful.

Life is very simple. You do what you do
until you do it no longer.

You can change if you want to change.

You can change if you need to change.

Change is necessary when you are not happy with your existence, when others are not happy with your actions, or when what you are doing is having a negative effect on yourself or those around you

Do your secrets die with you?

Religion is not fact. Religion is an opinion. If religion were fact, there would only be one religion.

If you give someone advice and they act upon that advice, you then become responsible for any karma that occurs due to your advice.

If I can help, I will help.

If I can make things better, I will make things better.

If I can do something good, I will do something good.

These should be the mantras of your life. Are they?

When survival is all that matters, what
does it matter?

If you see enlightenment as your goal and you are working towards it, you are missing the point of enlightenment.

Knowing there is nothing to know is the ultimate freedom.

Be free.

People always seem to have a reason for what they did and why. But reason rarely equals reality and all that is left is the aftermath.

What did you do to make today better?
Not just for you but for everyone.

Broken is never unbroken again.

There is always someone to blame.

It doesn't take that much more effort to
do things right.

Think about the words you have spoken and the actions you have unleashed. How would someone who does not know you describe you?

Instead of becoming angry at a person or at your life situation you should be angry at yourself for allowing a person or your life situation to make you angry.

Are you aware of your environment and the affect you having on it? Or, are you locked into a space of unawareness?

Every event in life gives you the chance to learn, grow, and change. How much are you letting yourself learn?

Do your friends tell you that what you did was okay when you know that it wasn't?

Do you remember the lies that you've
told?

How much time do you spend making excuses for your actions?

Why should you be forgiven?

For every bad thing you do there are repercussions.

For every person you hurt there are repercussions.

For every good thing you do there are repercussions.

For every person you help there are repercussions.

Remorse is only a valid emotion if you do something to fix what you have broken.

People who are nothing try to use the accomplishments of someone else to become something more.

What you choose to do either opens up new doors or puts another nail in your coffin.

What will be the definition of you?

There is no way to stop doing until you stop doing.

There is nobody to blame but you.

How is what you are doing today going to effect your tomorrow?

There is no person that is better than you.

The same old stories get old.

No Matter what your intentions, if what you did hurt anyone then your actions were wrong.

Life is measured by how much you laugh.

Optimism is the ultimate form of denial.

The accomplished are envied.

The benevolent are revered.

It's easy to criticize. It is much harder to create something better or do something more than what you are criticizing.

There is nothing godlike about making money off of religion or spirituality.

A Bad Person, who does a bad thing,
attempts to deny, rationalize, justify, or
even make excuses for their actions.

A Good Person, who does a bad thing,
does all that they can to repair any
damage they may have unleashed.

You don't repair your karma by doing something good for someone else. You repair your karma by repaying the person or persons that you wronged.

Did you think about you first or did you think about them?

Did you invade, take, use, break, steal to serve your own ends?

Did you hurt, damage, not think, not care?

When your life is being hurt, attacked, damaged, taken from are you upset?

Why do you do to others what you do not want done to you?

Here/Now is what you created with your life.

If you drive far enough on any highway
you can find what you're looking for.

You never care to care about anyone
unless they force their way into your life
in either a positive or negative manner.

How much are you thinking about what
you are doing before you are doing it?

The answer to that question is the
defining factor of your reality.

Desiring that you will...

Claiming that you will...

Does not equal accomplishment.

It only equals false promises.

The world is too full of false promises.

The claimers claim. The doers do.

When you have nothing to focus on, your
mind focuses on nothing.

When you are alone, you can only become angry with yourself.

If you are discussing what someone else has said that means that you have nothing of your own worth saying.

If you have broken or damaged someone or something you really need to fix it or the impact of what you have done will follow you forever.

If you want to fix your karma, go back to the beginning.

If you are silent no one can take issue
with your words.

Can you write your autobiography in one word?

This moment is your moment.

Listen for the silence.

If you do not take other people into consideration first – before you ever think about yourself, you have not earned the right to ever focus on how you are feeling.

There is no excuse for not having an excuse.

If you have no *Checks and Balances* then there are no *Checks and Balances*.

When you realize that it doesn't matter,
then you are free.

You don't actually believe that, do you?

Write a paragraph. Move the last sentence from the beginning to the end.

Is your meaning still present?

Paint a painting. Turn it upside down.

Is it still art?

Is it the truth or is it simply something that you believe?

If you don't try to fix what you have broken, it will remain forever broken.

The vain, the unconscious, and the angry
always make excuses for their actions.

If you have to sell yourself.

If you have to tell people who you are and what you are, you are nothing that you claim.

That is why the person who is true and whole onto themselves claims nothing.

They have nothing to prove to themselves or to others.

People want to believe in themselves.

People lie to themselves to justify their actions.

Do you?

Your life is defined by the existence you create.

Have you hurt people?

Have you helped people?

Look at where you are in your life and you will know the answer to those questions.

The world is full of people who are very self-involved and self-important.

Are you one of them?

Personal Realizations are defined by the word, *"Personal."*

Your realizations are not my realizations. Just as my realizations are not yours.

People may fight to spread the truth that they believe in. But, it is only the truth as they believe it.

The there is no one realization. There is no one truth.

Why do you want?

In life there is what you do and then there is what you want to do.

Your life is defined by those who surround you.

Describe yourself in one word.

How would other people describe you in one word?

You can be more but do you choose to be more?

The doer is always the one responsible
for what is done.

Who is responsible for your actions?

The root cause is you.

You business is your business, it only becomes my business when you make it that way.

What is your claim to fame?

Do you seek the positive or do you only embrace the negative?

Are your words excuses and justifications for your actions or are your words an expression of a deeper truth?

Scott Shaw Books-in-Print

*About Peace: A 103 Ways to Be At Peace
When Things Are Out of Control*

Advanced Taekwondo

Arc Left from Istanbul

Ballet for a Funeral

Bangkok and the Nights of Drunken Stupor

Bangkok: Beyond the Buddha

Bus Ride(s)

Cairo: Before the Aftermath

*Cambodian Refugees in Long Beach, California:
The Definitive Study*

Chi Kung For Beginners

China Deep

Echoes from Hell

Essence: The Zen of Everything

e.q.

Guangzhou: A Photographic Exploration

Hapkido: Articles on Self-Defense: Volume 1

Hapkido: Articles on Self-Defense: Volume 2

Hapkido: Essays on Self-Defense

Hapkido: The Korean Art of Self-Defense

Hong Kong: Out of Focus

Independent Filmmaking: Secrets of the Craft

In the Foreboding Shadows of Holiness

Israel in the Oblique

Junk: The Backstreets of Bangkok

Last Will and Testament According to the
        Divine Rites of the Drug Cocaine

L.A.: Tales from the Suburban Side of Hell

Los Angeles Skidrow: 1983

Marguerite Duras and Charles Bukowski:
The Yin and Yang of Modern Erotic Literature

Mastering Health: The A to Z of Chi Kung

Nirvana in a Nutshell

On the Hard Edge of Hollywood

Pagan, Burma: Shadows of the Stupa

Sake' in a Glass, Sushi with Your Fingers:
Fifteen Minutes in Tokyo

Scream of the Buddha

Scream: Southeast Asia and the Dream

Scribbles on the Restroom Wall

Samurai Zen

Sedona: Realm of the Vortex

Shama Baba

Shanghai Whispers Shanghai Screams

Shattered Thoughts

Singaore: Off Center

South Korea in a Blur

Suicide Slowly

Taekwondo Basics

Ten to Thirty

The Chronicles: Zen Ramblings from the Internet

The Ki Process: Korean Secrets for
        Cultivating Dynamic Energy